Wildlife of the Canadian Rockies

PHOTOGRAPHS AND TEXT BY WAYNE LYNCH

ASSISTED BY AUBREY LANG

Summerthought

Banff, Canada

WILDLIFE OF THE CANADIAN ROCKIES

Published by

Summerthought

Summerthought Publishing
PO Box 2309
Banff, AB T1L 1C1
Canada
www.summerthought.com

1st Edition—2010

Design and Production: Linda Petras
Printed in Canada by Friesens

We gratefully acknowledge the financial support of the Alberta Foundation for the Arts for our publishing activities.

Library and Archives Canada Cataloguing in Publication

Wayne Lynch
Wildlife of the Canadian Rockies / Wayne Lynch.

Includes index.
ISBN 978-0-9811491-3-4

1. Animals—Rocky Mountains, Canadian (B.C. and Alta.)—Pictorial works. 2. Rocky Mountains, Canadian (B.C. and Alta.)—Pictorial works. I. Title.

QL221.R6L963 2010   591.9711   C2009-907065-0

For Aubrey, my favourite hiking and backpacking companion.

Mother elk and calf

Great gray owl

CONTENTS

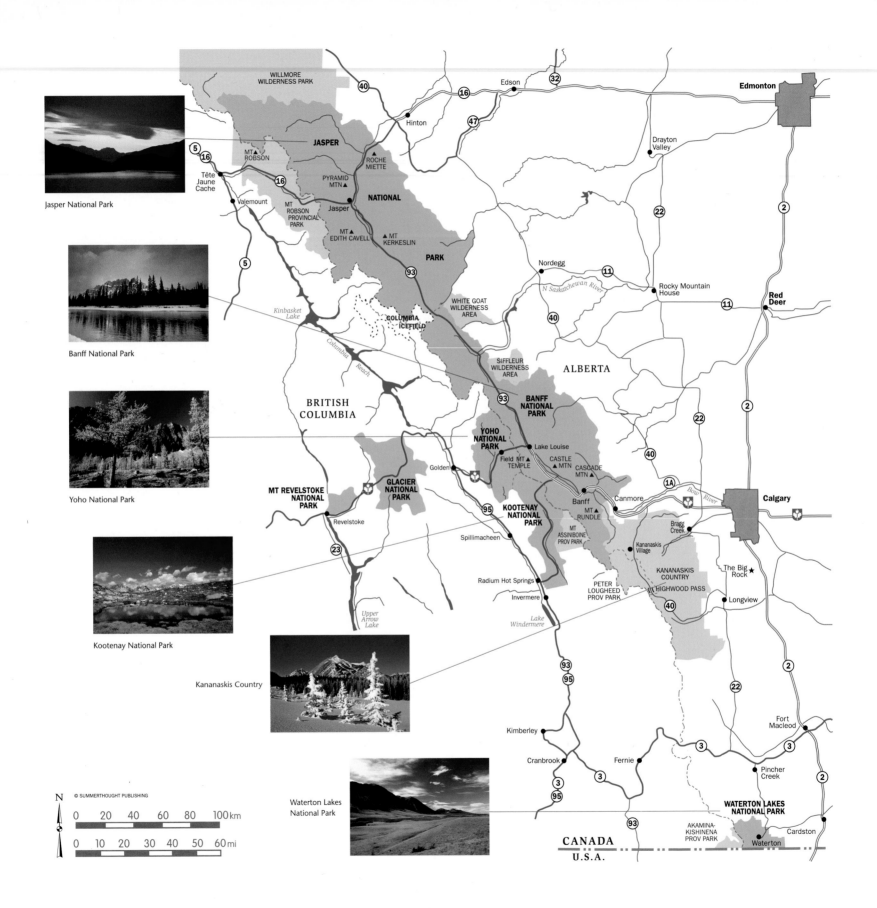

Jasper National Park

Banff National Park

Yoho National Park

Kootenay National Park

Kananaskis Country

Waterton Lakes National Park

WILLMORE WILDERNESS PARK

Edson

Edmonton

Hinton

Drayton Valley

JASPER

MT ROBSON

ROCHE MIETTE

PYRAMID MTN

NATIONAL

Jasper

Tête Jaune Cache

Valemount

MT ROBSON PROVINCIAL PARK

MT EDITH CAVELL

MT KERKESLIN

PARK

Nordegg

Rocky Mountain House

Red Deer

Kinbasket Lake

COLUMBIA ICEFIELD

WHITE GOAT WILDERNESS AREA

N Saskatchewan River

BRITISH COLUMBIA

Columbia Reach

SIFFLEUR WILDERNESS AREA

ALBERTA

BANFF NATIONAL PARK

YOHO NATIONAL PARK

Lake Louise

Golden

MT REVELSTOKE NATIONAL PARK

GLACIER NATIONAL PARK

Field

MT TEMPLE

CASTLE MTN

CASCADE MTN

Bow River

Calgary

Revelstoke

KOOTENAY NATIONAL PARK

Banff

MT RUNDLE

Canmore

Bragg Creek

Spillimacheen

MT ASSINIBOINE PROV PARK

Kananaskis Village

The Big Rock

Radium Hot Springs

Invermere

Upper Arrow Lake

Lake Windermere

PETER LOUGHEED PROV PARK

KANANASKIS COUNTRY

HIGHWOOD PASS

Longview

Kimberley

Fort Macleod

Cranbrook

Fernie

Pincher Creek

WATERTON LAKES NATIONAL PARK

AKAMINA-KISHINENA PROV PARK

Cardston

CANADA

U.S.A.

Waterton

N

© SUMMERTHOUGHT PUBLISHING

0   20   40   60   80   100 km

0   10   20   30   40   50   60 mi

INTRODUCTION

From my home in Calgary, Alberta, I can see the jagged peaks of the Canadian Rockies, 100 kilometres (60 miles) to the west. In moments of idle daydreaming, I often recall vivid memories from those snow-capped summits. I glimpse again the muscled shoulders of a bighorn sheep racing across a precipitous cliff in BANFF NATIONAL PARK. One winter not too long ago, I remember watching a trio of wolves as they loped across the frozen surface of a river in JASPER NATIONAL PARK, then in fall the rubbery lips of a black bear in KOOTENAY NATIONAL PARK as it stripped berries from a roadside bush. At other times, I recollect the delightful camouflage of a clutch of ptarmigan chicks in an alpine meadow in KANANASKIS COUNTRY, the comical contortions of a hoary marmot tormented by mosquitoes in YOHO NATIONAL PARK, or the buoyant flight of a great horned owl as it melted into a thicket of aspens in WATERTON LAKES NATIONAL PARK. My memories of the Canadian Rockies always include wildlife. It is muscle and blood, feathers and fur, that gives these mountains their life force, and it is the wildlife which makes the Canadian Rockies so compelling to visit and rewarding to explore.

The Rocky Mountains are one of the longest mountain chains on Earth, stretching 3,100 kilometres (1,926 miles) from northern British Columbia to southern New Mexico. The Rockies are their most majestic as they forge across western Canada, dividing the provinces of Alberta and British Columbia.

With such length and height, the Canadian Rockies are biologically diverse. Even a half-day hike from valley bottom to the tree line will introduce the visitor to dramatically changing vegetation and climate. (An elevation gain of 300 metres/1,000 feet made on the flank of a mountain is roughly the same as a northward trek of 1,600 kilometres/1,000 miles).

While local ecosystems include rocky summits, evergreen forests, flower-filled alpine meadows, aspen woodlands, rivers and lakes, and open grasslands, I have arranged the portfolio of wildlife photographs into three general habitats. In the Wetlands chapter I focus on the lakes, ponds, rivers, and streams. The Foothills chapter explores the richness of the aspen and lodgepole pine forests that skirt the bottoms of the higher slopes. In the High Country chapter, I concentrate on the subalpine forests and the alpine zone stretching beyond the tree line. Naturally, these three divisions are artificial. An animal placed in the foothills chapter, for example, may also be found in the high country, or the wetlands or both. Generally, I tried to showcase the wildlife in the habitat most important to them.

Canada geese

Wildlife of the Canadian Rockies is my tribute to the magnificent and the mighty, the elegant and the elusive. In your travels through the Canadian Rockies, I hope you will discover, as I have, the beauty and magic of its wild creatures.

WETLANDS

etlands are one of the best places in the Canadian Rockies to see wildlife. DUCKS, LOONS, and CANADA GEESE use lakes to court and casually loaf. The thick snarl of bushes lining the edges of streams and rivers attract foraging BEAVERS, MINK, and MUSKRATS. The largest mammal of the wetlands is the MOOSE, an antlered member of the deer family that is relatively rare, but with a range that extends throughout the Canadian Rockies. Here also, innumerable SONGBIRDS search the tangles for food, finding safety from fast-flying birds of prey in the jumble of branches and leaves. In wetlands, one never knows when a BALD EAGLE or OSPREY may suddenly swoop overhead. Expect the unexpected.

Recently in Jasper National Park, I spent several hours hidden beside a marsh atop an abandoned beaver dam to watch the wetland awaken with the sun. At first, the skies were clouded and I resigned myself to a morning of wildlife-watching without taking too many photos. As is often said in the mountains, if you don't like the weather, just wait ten minutes. Suddenly, the clouds split apart and beams of amber light bathed the surrounding mountains with a Midas touch. As the sunlight shone across the marsh, the thin bank of fog that hung over the water was instantly transformed into a golden gossamer veil. In the magical hours that followed, I watched a trio of

male ring-necked ducks court a reluctant hen with vociferous enthusiasm. From the cluttered shoreline next to me, the plaintive whinny of a sora rail rose from the greenery, and moments later this secretive bird swam in front of me, its reflection a perfect mirror image. The longer I sat, the more I noticed the sights and sounds of the wetland world around me: a pair of Canada geese squabbling from the far shore, a male cinnamon teal preening in a tangle of sedges, a courting snipe winnowing overhead, the muffled drumming of a ruffed grouse from the forested shadows behind me, and a solitary muskrat unhurriedly etching a silver line across the glassy surface of the water as it swam to its burrow hidden under a clump of willows.

In quiet times like these, my mind sometimes wanders on flights of unexpected reflection. Consider a single drop of meltwater that drips from the lip of a glacier high among the peaks of the Canadian Rockies. The droplet is joined by others and becomes a trickle, then a stream, and finally a tumbling river empties into a quiet lake, tinted like polished jade. At the far end of the lake the droplets are carried into other rivers, and from there into marshes, lakes, and still larger rivers until finally the mountains are left behind. In the journey from mountain peaks to valley lowlands, the wetlands of the Canadian Rockies have many different faces. Look for water and you will find life.

Osprey

Moose

A bull moose reaches its maximum body and antler size when it is between eight and 12 years of age. A prime bull may weigh over 450 kilograms (990 pounds), and carry a massive 27-kilogram (60-pound) palmate rack that spans nearly two metres (six feet) from tip to tip.

PREVIOUS PAGES

Although all moose need sodium, the demands of pregnancy and nursing mean females require twice as much salt as males. Aquatic plants such as yellow water lilies, bladderwort, and green alga are especially rich in salt. For over two hours, I watched this cow moose dredge the lake bottom for salt-rich plants.

Moose

Moose calves, often twins, are born in late May or early June. For the first week after birth, a mother moose rarely strays farther than 50 metres (160 feet) from her calves, and she may keep her offspring sequestered in the seclusion of the birthing area for up to three weeks.

Moose

These calves are roughly three months old. The first few months in a calf's life is the most vulnerable time, with predators such as grizzlies and black bears posing the greatest threat. Mothers can use their heavy, sharp front hooves to protect their offspring.

Mink

The mink is a generalist hunter that scours the banks of shallow, slow-moving streams and rivers and the vegetated shorelines of sloughs, lakes, and ponds searching for crustaceans, amphibians, insects, and small mammals.

Bald eagle OPPOSITE

In the Canadian Rockies, the bald eagle feeds mainly on fish. It is a frugal sit-and-wait hunter, perching beside rivers and lakes while scanning the water for a ripple, a fin, or the pallid flash of a fish corpse driven ashore by the wind.

Canada geese

Typically, Canada geese lay four to seven eggs. Once the goslings hatch, dominant adults may adopt additional chicks from other pairs. Since the goslings feed themselves, this imposes no hardship on the adoptive parents, who benefit by having the predation risk on their own chicks lessened by the added number of young.

Canada geese

Canada geese are some of the earliest waterfowl to return to the mountains in spring, often arriving in early April when the lakes are still largely covered with ice. When food is scarce they rely on the fat reserves they accumulated over the winter.

Common goldeneye

The goldeneye is a diving duck that feeds on leeches, frogs, and aquatic insects, as well as plant material such as pondweeds. It is a fast-flying bird whose wings make a whistling sound, earning it the nickname of "whistler." The male pictured here was feeding along the melting edge of a frozen lake.

Common loon

The haunting, quavering yodel of the loon echoes across the still waters of lakes throughout the Canadian Rockies. The origin of the name loon was an old Norse word, *lom,* meaning lame, a reference to the awkward way these birds move on land because of the extreme rearward position of their legs.

Horned grebe

The horned grebe builds a waterlogged platform of floating weeds on which it lays its eggs. A pair may build a nest in just three hours, but usually adds more material later. Both the male and female share in incubating the eggs.

Harlequin duck
The turbulent waters of rushing mountain rivers and streams are the favoured haunt of the distinctively patterned harlequin duck. The strikingly feathered drake, pictured here, arrives in the Canadian Rockies in April and may leave again for the Pacific coast as early as July, where it spends the winter.

American avocets

t's late May and these avocets are courting. The female, easily identified by a greater curve in her bill, is in the rear. Avocets usually form pairs on their Mexican wintering grounds or during spring migration. Upon returning to the Canadian Rockies, each pair stakes out and defends a small feeding territory.

Pied-billed grebe OPPOSITE

The pied-billed grebe is heard far more often than it is seen. The male's territoria song is a loud, throaty *kow, kow, kow,* which can be heard up to one kilometre (0.6 miles) away. The loud call penetrates the thick stands of marsh vegetation where these birds live, and their courtship consists mainly of vocal displays

Red-necked grebe
The position of the red-necked grebe's legs at the back of its body gives it power and manoeuvrability underwater. Because its legs are so far to the rear, it walks with difficulty, and it is almost impossible for it to take off from land. This bird is mounting its floating nest.

River otter

Inhabiting the Columbia River wetlands, but rarely seen by casual observers, the river otter is a fish-catching specialist. Its thick pelt traps an insulating layer of air next to its skin that keeps the animal warm, even in icy waters.

Beaver OPPOSITE

The beaver does not hibernate for the winter. To sustain it through the season when lakes and ponds are frozen, it caches surplus food during warmer months. A beaver family may stash up to 325 kilograms (720 pounds) of alder, willow, and red-osier dogwood branches in a single pile.

Muskrat

As soon as a muskrat dives into ice-cold water, its body begins to cool. To prolong the time it has for foraging before it must retreat to its lodge to warm up, muskrats actively boost their body temperature by a degree or two before they go diving.

Muskrats
Unlike the beaver that stores a cache of food in advance of winter, muskrats live from day to day. In winter, they leave the warmth and security of their lodge to forage underwater for the buried roots of cattails, bulrushes, sedges, and horsetails. Sometimes they may dig through 50 centimetres (20 inches) of mud to uncover a juicy root.

Boreal chorus frog

The boreal chorus frog adopts a drastic strategy to survive the winter—it freezes itself, turning as much as two-thirds of the water in its body to ice. During this time, it stops breathing and it has no heartbeat. When spring returns, the frog's body slowly warms, the ice melts, and it miraculously comes back to life.

Damselflies

These handsome damselflies are at the beginning of courtship. The pair may stay attached like this for hours and fly around together until the female finally lays her eggs in a shallow patch of water.

Dragonfly
The variable darner, pictured, is one of the large dragonflies that commonly occur around lakes in the Canadian Rockies. This fast-flying insect is a voracious predator of mosquitoes. It may eat three hundred or more in a day, earning it the well-deserved nickname "mosquito hawk".

FOOTHILLS

The lower slopes of the Canadian Rockies are known as the foothills. Here, the forests often mix with open meadows and grasslands, and the trees are spaced farther apart than they are at higher elevations. Open spaces in the foothills are a good place to search for wildlife. Smaller mammals, such as GROUND SQUIRRELS, are common throughout this ecosystem and most often seen at picnic areas and campgrounds. ELK, DEER, COYOTES, BLACK BEARS, and RED FOXES can be seen throughout the day by casual observers, but all become more active as the sun begins to set. Birdlife is more prolific than the casual observer may imagine. Owls have always been one of my favourite photographic subjects, and as you'll see in the following pages, many species make the foothills region their home, including the GREAT HORNED OWL, which has been designated as Alberta's provincial bird.

If you want the ultimate exercise workout, then follow a researcher trying to keep up with a pack of bloodhounds trailing a healthy COUGAR through the foothills of the Canadian Rockies. I did this one winter in Kananaskis Country. The biologists I was working with wanted to learn what these wild cats were hunting, and how often they killed for food. I soon learned that cougar researchers are different than regular folks. Their hearts beat only once an hour, they climb steep hills with unexplained glee, and they never stop to eat, drink or catch their breath. Three hours and six hills later, we finally crossed a cougar track that was fresh enough to unleash the dogs. Within moments, the baying blue tick hounds were distant echoes, compelling us to follow. As we plodded after the dogs, the researchers reminisced about former cougar chases, the excitement of pursuit, and the exhilaration of captures. Even the bitter bite of defeat by wily felines with names like Phantom and Mirage were memories to relish. By late afternoon, when it seemed I had died a dozen times, the hounds finally treed the cougar. The 40-kilogram (88-pound) cat was remarkably calm, but glared at us from the branch of a lodgepole pine, eight metres (26 feet) overhead. A few minutes later, a tranquillizing dart was fired into the animal's left hip and soon the cat was unconscious on the ground next to us. It is a rare privilege to see a wild cougar on a tree branch, but it is even better to see it closely on the ground and touch its wildness.

Cougar

Coyote

Smaller than a wolf but larger than a red fox, the coyote originally lived only in prairie grasslands east of the Rocky Mountains. In the 1800s, as wolves were systematically exterminated, the adaptable coyote moved in to fill the void. It now ranges from Alaska to Costa Rica and from the Pacific to the Atlantic Oceans.

OPPOSITE One author quipped "the coyote's favourite food is anything it can chew." This particular animal was hunting voles in a grassy meadow beside the highway.

Mule deer

Mule deer are born at the end of May in a secluded patch of forest. For several weeks, a newborn fawn will remain hidden in a spot of its own choosing, revealing itself only when its mother returns from foraging for her own food.

Mule deer

Sparring is a way for young mule deer bucks to evaluate their own size and rank against that of rivals. The animals carefully lock antlers then push and twist, attempting to knock their opponent off balance. These short matches usually last less than one minute.

Cougar

Unlike all other large mammals in the mountains, a cougar may breed at any time of the year. In fact, a number of births occur in winter, seemingly the most demanding of seasons. A female cougar may have one to three kittens. This young animal is three to four months old.

Elk

Elk are the most common large mammal in the Canadian Rockies. A bull elk usually sheds its antlers from the previous year in February and a new set begins to grow almost immediately. The antlers are full grown by early August, in anticipation of the fall rut.

Black bear

This subadult black bear is around 18 months old and probably only recently separated from its mother. Black bears evolved in a forested environment and climbing to safety is still one of their initial reactions to danger.

OPPOSITE The black bear comes in a number of colour variations. As many as 40% of black bears in the Canadian Rockies are some shade of brown, ranging from cinnamon to dark chocolate. This bear was eating dandelions and horsetails by the roadside.

Black bear
This black bear cub is roughly three months old and had two siblings. The number of cubs in a litter depends mainly upon the mother's nutrition. In years when berries are abundant and a female gains considerable weight she may give birth to a large litter. Otherwise, one or two cubs is typical.

Great gray owl

Winter is the best season in which to observe and enjoy the behaviour of the great gray owl. This owl is a sit-and-wait predator. Typically, it perches in a tree on the edge of a clearing and waits for a hapless rodent to reveal itself.

Great horned owl
The great horned owl is the largest and most powerful owl living in the Canadian Rockies. Its primary prey are squirrels, snowshoe hares, and ruffed grouse. The great horned owl can be identified by its fluffy ear tufts and bright yellow eyes.

Great horned owl

A mother great horned owl usually raises two to four chicks. These young owls are a little over three weeks old. They will stay in their nest until they are five or six weeks of age and then disperse to nearby branches where the parents will continue to feed them for several more months.

Northern saw-whet owl

This northern saw-whet owl was hunting redpolls and chickadees at a backyard feeder near Hinton, Alberta, east of Jasper National Park. The unwary owl allowed me to get within a few metres of it without becoming frightened.

Ruffed grouse

In spring, the male ruffed grouse advertises its presence by noisily beating its wings while perching on a fallen tree trunk. If an interested female appears, the grouse enhances its appeal by fanning its tail and flaring the feathered ruff around its neck.

Swainson's hawk

This Swainson's hawk has its wings extended to dry its feathers after it was soaked in a rainstorm. The bird is a juvenile, recently independent from its parents. Swainson's hawks make the longest winter migration of any hawk in North America, flying to Argentina.

Swainson's hawk

Swainson's hawks live and nest on the edge of the foothills next to the
prairies. They compete with the more forest-adapted red-tailed hawk.

Columbian ground squirrel

The Columbian ground squirrel lives in colonies. It is a large squirrel that takes two years to reach full adult size. Males disperse from their natal colony in their second summer of life, whereas females tend to remain close to where they were born.

Badger OPPOSITE

The badger is a burrowing member of the Weasel Family. It feeds mainly on ground squirrels and pocket gophers that it hunts in grassy areas. The badger can be active throughout the winter, but when food is scarce or the weather conditions severe, it can lapse into lethargy and may stay underground for days or weeks at a time.

Richardson's ground squirrel
It is mid-summer and this female Richardson's ground squirrel is already preparing the nest where she will hibernate. Provided they have accumulated the necessary fat reserves to see them through the winter, females may go into hibernation as early as July.

Richardson's ground squirrel

Richardson's ground squirrels emerge from winter hibernation in February, a sure sign that spring is on the way. Adult males, sex-starved and pugnacious, surface first. Adult females come up two weeks later and usually mate on their third day out.

Wolf

A wolf may howl at any time of day and in any season. A wolf will howl for a number of reasons: to locate pack members when it has strayed from them, to advertise the occupancy of a defended territory, and to intimidate rival neighbours, warning them not to trespass.

OPPOSITE Wolf populations in the Canadian Rockies have fluctuated greatly in the last century. It is estimated that around only 10 to 12 packs are currently present in the four contiguous national parks, which makes seeing this fabled creature in the wild a real thrill.

Short-tailed weasel

The short-tailed weasel, or ermine, is the tiny terror of the mountains. This 70-gram (2.5-oz) lightweight hunts voles, mice, pikas, and ground squirrels. The weasel's long slender body allows it to tunnel beneath the snow and pursue prey along its own runway.

Red fox
The russet-coloured red fox is commonly sighted in roadside ditches and grassy meadows throughout the Canadian Rockies. Weighing just four to seven kilograms (nine to 15 pounds), it hunts voles, squirrels, and grouse, but also eats berries and some insects.

HIGH COUNTRY

The high country is an arbitrary designation that includes two distinct habitats. The subalpine, or the "snow forest," is where trees grow close together and the environment is often cool, shaded and fragrant. Alpine, the land above tree line, covers the largest area of the Canadian Rockies. For example, in Banff and Jasper the alpine zone covers more than half the parks' total area. The alpine is one of my favourite places in the Canadian Rockies for wildlife viewing and photography. With no trees to hide the view, you can watch GRIZZLY BEARS digging for roots, HOARY MARMOTS whistling from rocky slopes, and nimble MOUNTAIN GOATS balancing on precipitous cliffs. For many visitors, the lower elevations of high country provide prime wildlife viewing with little or no effort. BIGHORN SHEEP and ELK are commonly seen from roadways throughout the Canadian Rockies, while birds such as the cheeky CLARK'S NUTCRACKER are easily spied at picnic areas.

Can a bird feel embarrassment? The scientist in me suspects it probably cannot, but in a recent spring time photography session I watched a SPRUCE GROUSE that may have come as close as it possibly could to this uncomfortable human emotion. Having previous experience with the birds' unwariness, on this particular trip I brought a stuffed female grouse with me to see how a hormone-charged male would react. My target was a male I had been photographing for several days. As soon as I found him, I placed the alluring female on the ground and laid down close by to watch the show. In a heartbeat, the male was next to us. His tail was fanned, his neck feathers flared, and his eye combs engorged a brilliant scarlet. He had a single thought in his tiny brain and my closeness to him seemed unimportant. He was so unconcerned by me that I tapped him on the rump several times to nudge him into better light. The frozen pose of the stuffed female didn't deter his ardour for an instant, and after a couple of minutes of parading and swaggering he promptly hopped on her back. To steady himself, he drooped his wings, grasped the feathers on the nape of her neck with his beak, and tread backwards carefully to position himself. Just as he was about to make his final move, the female's head tore loose. The male jerked upright in surprise, still holding the head in his beak with cotton stuffing hanging out the bottom of it. He immediately jumped off and looked around nervously. If he could have spoken, I'm sure he would have pleaded "It wasn't me. Really, it wasn't. Honest, I didn't do anything." At this point, he was still holding the incriminating head in his beak as if he didn't know what to do with it. After a second or so, he dropped it, glanced quickly at the headless female, and ran into the forest. I never saw him again.

Mountain goat

Grizzly bear

After being tranquillized by a biologist, I was able to measure the front claws on this grizzly bear. The distance along the outside curve of its longest claw was 14 centimetres (5.5 inches), which is the length of a pen.

OPPOSITE The conspicuous shoulder hump on a grizzly bear is one of the best ways to distinguish it from a brown-coloured black bear. The hump is a mass of muscle the bear uses to power its front limbs when it digs for roots and ground squirrels.

Grizzly bear

These four-month-old grizzly cubs will stay with
their mother for two and half years. For the first six
to eight months of their lives, they will rely on their
mother's milk for the bulk of their nutrition. After that,
they will eat greenery, roots, and berries, while also
scavenging elk or moose kills that their mother makes.

Spruce grouse

In courtship, the male spruce grouse struts about and alternately fans one side of his tail, then the other, giving the appearance of swaying. As his tail feathers rub against each other, they produce a quiet swishing sound.

Dusky grouse

The colourful areas of bare skin on the neck and above the eyes of the male dusky grouse signifies the male's health and vitality. Unhealthy males—ones that forage poorly or are infected with parasites—are less brightly coloured. Biologists believe that female grouse use such colourful cues to evaluate the desirability of potential partners.

Bighorn sheep

In winter, bighorn sheep of all ages and sexes may sometimes forage together. It is more usual, however, for ewes and lambs to overwinter in separate areas from those used by large mature rams. This photograph was taken early in winter, before the two groups had moved to different wintering areas.

Elk

Elk calves are born in May, weighing 10 to 20 kilograms (22 to 45 pounds) at birth. For the first few weeks of their life, they stay hidden in secluded areas, away from other elk. This isolation gives the mother and newborn time to imprint on each other.

OPPOSITE At around three weeks of age, a mother may introduce her calf to other mothers with calves, forming small cow-calf herds. In the Canadian Rockies, these herds typically contain less than a dozen animals.

Elk

None of the Deer Family have front teeth in their upper jaw, as you can clearly see in this photograph of a bugling bull elk. In fall bull elk bugle to advertise their vigour and whereabouts. A high ranking bull may bugle as often as 48 times in 30 minutes. The more vigorous a bull bugles the more females he can attract to his harem.

Elk

Deep snow is a hardship for elk. They must paw through it to reach the grasses they like to eat. Because elk tend to drag their feet, they also burn valuable energy reserves moving about. As snow accumulates in the high country, elk migrate to lower elevations and are often seen in the towns of Banff and Jasper.

Pine grosbeak

The large conical beak on the male pine grosbeak identifies it as a seed eater.
In winter, grosbeaks are extremely gregarious and commonly travel in flocks
of a dozen or two. Sometimes a group may number more than 100 birds.

Boreal owls OPPOSITE

Newly hatched boreal owl chicks have a coat of whitish down when they first break out of
the egg. Within a few weeks, their natal coat is replaced by a second downy coat. Young
owls would not normally huddle together like this; these chicks were being banded.

Caribou

The woodland caribou is a subspecies of caribou that ranges across much of the forested and mountainous regions of Canada. In the Canadian Rockies, the caribou occurs in small numbers and is an endangered species. The recent decline in the caribou population results, in a large part, from the loss and fragmentation of habitat combined with increased predation by wolves.

Mountain goats

A mother mountain goat will stay with her kid for up to a year. Even though mountains goats spend most of their time on high cliffs, visitors see them at roadside salt licks, which the animals visit in spring and early summer.

OPPOSITE The mountain goat is the most skilled rock climber in the Canadian Rockies. The shaggy beast moves with agility and confidence along ledges so narrow it seems impossible for the animal to pass. It displays equal nimbleness in leaping from ledge to ledge.

Mountain bluebird
The colours in a bird's feathers are usually produced by pigments. It is different for the male mountain bluebird, whose brilliant colouration results from the optical effects of light on the microscopic structure of the feathers.

Clark's nutcracker

The Clark's nutcracker has an exceptional memory for a so-called birdbrain. In fall, the nutcracker may stash tens of thousands of pine seeds for later retrieval, remembering most of the locations, even when they are buried under snow.

Northern flying squirrel

Because of its nocturnal habits, the northern flying squirrel is rarely seen. It spends the daylight hours hidden in tree cavities. The squirrel doesn't actually fly, but glides using stretched folds of skin along the sides of its body. The squirrel's large tail is helpful in steering.

Gray jay OPPOSITE

The bold, inquisitive gray jay is the earliest songbird to nest in the mountains. Most are warming eggs by the end of March, when temperatures are still frigid. The jays build a thick nest of shredded bark, twigs, and lichens and insulate it with hundreds of grouse feathers.

Golden-mantled ground squirrel

The golden-mantled ground squirrel, often mistaken for a large chipmunk, is the most strikingly coloured squirrel in the Canadian Rockies. The handsome squirrels readily accept handouts of food from campers and picnickers and quickly become unwary. Even so, feeding any animal in a national park is illegal.

Lynx

The lynx is primarily an ambush hunter of hares. A study in Alberta showed that once a lynx surprises its prey, a successful chase is over in just seven jumps across 12 metres (39 feet). Even so, the hare outruns the lynx in five chases out of six.

Hoary marmot
The hoary marmot, weighing up to 8.5 kilograms (19 pounds), is the largest squirrel in North America. Its large size is an adaptation for life at high altitudes where temperatures can be cool, even in the summer months. The marmot may spend two-thirds of its life in hibernation.

Pika
Around one quarter the size of a marmot, the pika looks like a guinea pig, although it's not a rodent at all but a lagomorph—the same family as rabbits and hares. The pika's family ties, as well as its choice of habitat, have earned it the popular name rock rabbit.

Porcupine

Baby porcupines are generally born in May. A newborn porcupine, called a porcupette, is precocious at birth. Its eyes are open, its teeth erupted, and its body protected by splinter-sized quills that harden within an hour.

Fisher

The fisher is an arboreal member of the Weasel Family. Its greatest claim to fame is its ability to successfully prey on porcupines, something few other mountain predators do. No one is certain how the fisher got its common name since it does not fish. More commonly it hunts grouse, hares and squirrels.

Bighorn sheep

The horns on a bighorn sheep are the easiest way to age the animal. The sheep pictured here is an adult female whose horns grow very little once she reaches adulthood. The horns on a ram continue to grow until the animal is eight or nine years old. By that age, their horns are massive and curl around below the animal's eye level.

WILDLIFE VIEWING TIPS

Catching a glimpse of an animal or a bird in the wild can often be a matter of luck, of being in the right place at the right time. Even so, you can increase your chances of successfully finding and viewing wildlife by using a few simple tips that have been helpful for me over three decades of exploring the Canadian Rockies.

Learn About Your Subject

There is no point looking for a marmot in the foothills or for a black bear in the alpine zone. To be successful at finding wildlife, a good strategy is to become a nature nerd. Before I go searching for any wild animal or bird I visit a bookstore or the library, or search on the Internet to find out as much information as I can. I try to learn where an animal normally lives, when it is most active, its diet, and where it searches for food. I also want to know when an animal is likely to be most disturbed by my presence and I stay away at those times. For example, nesting birds and animals such as red foxes and wolves raising their young at a den site should never be disturbed. As well, if an animal is potentially dangerous, I want to know if there are times when I might be at risk for injury and should search for another subject. Numerous wildlife enthusiasts have been injured when they foolishly tried to get a closer look at a newborn elk or moose calf.

Dusk and Dawn Rewards

If you want to see wildlife in its natural habitat, don't plan on too many lazy mornings in bed. Wildlife is often most active in the hours around sunrise. In the Canadian Rockies during the summer months, that can mean dragging your weary body out of bed at five a.m. The rewards will hopefully justify the effort. If you do sleep in, you'll have a second chance at the end of the day. Many nocturnal animals and birds start to stir before the sun sets, so try to be out and about in the early hours of twilight.

Move Slowly and Indirectly

Once you catch sight of an animal or bird, you can try moving closer. Make sure your subject sees you—otherwise it may be startled when you suddenly pop up, and it will most certainly flee. To get closer, take an indirect course. Move slowly and in small increments. Perhaps, pretend to be walking past your subject rather than directly towards it? The less you behave like a predator, the more likely you are to get near.

By moving slowly I got very close to this white-tailed ptarmigan.

It's possible to see more than 250 species of birds in the Canadian Rockies.

Finally, and most importantly, always give animals a way to retreat.

Sit Down and Stay Quiet

Suppose you find a lake, stream, or beaver pond with animal tracks leading to the water's edge and along the shore. This is the perfect location to sit against a tree trunk to partially camouflage your outline and wait to see who comes along. Animals and birds will soon recover from the disturbance of your arrival and you'll catch yourself detecting subtle sounds and smells that you never noticed upon your arrival. By sitting quietly, I've had close encounters with hunting weasels, swimming river otters, busy beavers, thirsty moose with their calves, and innumerable curious ducks and loons.

Carry Binoculars

Binoculars allow a person to get intimate views of animal behaviour without needing to be too close, but there is nothing more frustrating than to see a bird and not be able to find it through your binoculars. Therefore, if you are not familiar with using binoculars, practice at home so that you can learn how to aim them and focus on a target. For beginners, I would suggest a pair that is six or eight power in strength. I use a pair of Nikon binoculars that cost around $150 and weighs only 125 grams (1/4 pound).

Become a Wildlife Detective

On many wildlife-viewing trips I come home empty-handed, but I'm never disappointed that I went looking. The reason? Discovering the secret lives of Canadian Rockies wildlife can be as rewarding as seeing the animal or bird itself. Over the years, I've become pretty good at identifying tracks, scats, feeding signs, rub trees, and various other signs of wildlife. Animal signs help me to uncover an animal's behaviour and get a glimpse into its life. On top of that, it enriches the experience and adds depth and insight to an outing.

Be Patient

Even in the Canadian Rockies, where wildlife is abundant, patience is needed for wildlife viewing. The images showcased in this book were taken over a period of 30 years, so don't expect to see a great variety of species in a short space of time.

ETHICAL WILDLIFE VIEWING IN THE CANADIAN ROCKIES

- Give wildlife plenty of space.
- Don't feed wildlife, even if it comes begging for food.
- Don't whistle or throw rocks to get an animal's attention.
- If you see an animal while driving, don't stop in the middle of the road.
- Leave pets at home, or at the very least keep dogs on a leash when hiking.
- Avoid surprising wildlife by making noise when hiking.
- Stay clear of nests and younger animals.
- Check at visitor centres for trail closures due to wildlife activity.

INDEX